How Do You Investigate?

 HOUGHTON MIFFLIN HARCOURT

Printed in Mexico

ISBN: 978-0-544-07208-4

8 9 10 0908 21 20 19 18 17

4500665195   A B C D E F G

Look for each word in yellow along with its meaning.

senses

investigation

science tools

thermometer

inquiry skills

Underlined sentences answer these questions.

What are the five senses?

How do you use your senses?

What happens when you observe?

What do scientists do?

What is a science tool?

How can you record what you learn?

How do you use inquiry skills?

What are the five senses?

Senses help you learn about the world. You have five senses. You can see and hear. You can taste and smell. You can touch things.

You can taste your food.

How do you use your senses?

You see with your eyes. You hear with your ears. You smell with your nose. You taste food with your mouth. You touch with your hands.

see

hear

smell

taste

touch

This child is watching a man play with his dog.

What happens when you observe?

Watch! You can observe things happen. When you watch something, you observe it. You can observe a bird flying in the sky.

What do scientists do?

Scientists ask questions about what they see. They look for answers. Sometimes they plan a test called an investigation.

What does a plant need to grow? A scientist can try to find out.

A scientist can investigate the needs of plants.

water in sun, water in shade

You can ask a science question to learn more about something.

Does the sun help make water warm? You can use tools and numbers to get an answer.

What is a science tool?

Science tools help you learn more about things. A thermometer is a science tool. A thermometer tells how hot or cold something is. A thermometer uses numbers.

A measuring cup is a science tool that measures liquids. It uses numbers, too.

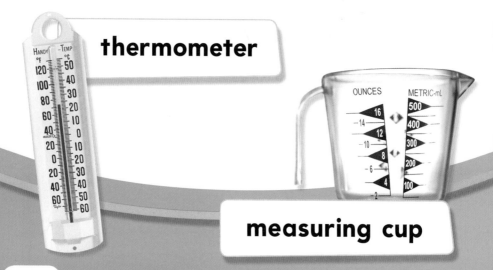

thermometer

measuring cup

How can you record what you learn?

Take the temperature of the water in each cup. Write down the time. Write down the number on the thermometer.

This chart shows how it can be done.

Time	Cup 1 (Sun)	Cup 2 (Shade)
11:00	33 °F	33 °F
11:30	37 °F	35 °F
12:00	43 °F	40 °F
12:30	50 °F	47 °F
1:00	65 °F	56 °F
1:30	72 °F	60 °F
2:00	75 °F	62 °F

It is important to write down what you learn.

What does the chart show?

Look! The water got warmer in both cups. The water in the sun is the warmest.

Time	Cup 1 (Sun)	Cup 2 (Shade)
11:00	33 °F	33 °F
11:30	37 °F	35 °F
12:00	43 °F	40 °F
12:30	50 °F	47 °F
1:00	65 °F	56 °F
1:30	72 °F	60 °F
2:00	75 °F	62 °F

Inquiry Skills

observe ✔

ask a science question ✔

plan an investigation ✔

measure ✔

compare ✔

predict -- say what you think will happen ✔

How do you use inquiry skills?

You use inquiry skills when you observe. You use them to ask questions. You use inquiry skills when you look for answers. Inquiry skills help you find out information.

Stay Safe!

Some science tools are safer to use than others. How can we stay safe when we use science tools? Work with a friend. Think of ways to stay safe when using science tools.

 Write it down

Predict how many dogs you will see today. Write down when, where, and how many you see. Put the numbers in a chart. Compare your information with a classmate's information.